Purrfectly Pawsome:
Tales From a Cat Sitter

J. S. Brown

First published in 2024 by Blossom Spring Publishing
Purrfectly Pawsome: Tales From a Cat Sitter
Copyright © 2024 Jillian Brown
ISBN 978-1-0686195-5-7
E: admin@blossomspringpublishing.com
W: www.blossomspringpublishing.com

I would like to express my gratitude to all those who have supported me throughout my journey, including my husband, friends, and family. I would like to give a special thanks to my friends Tricia and June, who provided me with valuable feedback.

Additionally, I am grateful to Graeme Sherriff, BVM&S, MRCVS, for reviewing my manuscript and providing me with his positive professional feedback. Thank you all for believing in me and helping me reach this point.

Purrfectly Pawsome:
Tales From a Cat Sitter

I'm a cat sitter based in West Lothian. I would like to share some of my stories, knowledge (with behaviours and what I have experienced through my journey); hopefully, it'll help understand our little feline companions a bit more, hints and tips from where it all began with my love of cats and how it led to me starting my cat sitting service to where I am now. My book is a must for all cat owners and lovers.

Setting up a business can be challenging, but with proper planning and organisation, it can be a rewarding experience. One of the most important aspects of starting a cat sitting service is a clear understanding of your target market and the services you will offer. You should also consider the legal requirements of starting a business in your area and ensure that you have all the necessary licences and permits (this does not apply in the UK). As a cat sitter, you may encounter various behaviours from cats, such as aggression or hiding. Being patient and giving the cat time to warm up to you is important. You can also suggest the use of pheromone sprays or diffusers to help calm the cat and create a more relaxed environment for the owner to consider. In addition to providing food, water, and litter box maintenance, you may also need to administer medications or provide basic grooming services. It's important to clearly understand the cat's needs and any medical conditions they may have. Communication is key when it comes to providing excellent service to your clients. Make sure to have clear communication with the cat owner about their expectations and any special instructions for caring for their cat. Keeping a detailed log of each visit can also help ensure consistency and provide peace of mind for the owner. Overall, starting a cat sitting business can be a rewarding experience for cat lovers. With proper planning, organisation, and a love for feline friends, you can provide a valuable service to cat owners and their furry companions.

1. Background and where it all began
2. My cats and some introduction tips
3. Starting up and being self-employed
4. The competitors
5. The customer base
6. Kitties and behaviour
7. Pheromones
8. Indoors or outdoors
9. The struggle is real and pet bereavement
10. Cuddles and more
11. The onward journey

1

Background and where it all began

I have been a cat lover for as long as I can remember. When I was little and growing up, my family always had cats — there was a cat called Blacky (before I was born).

My family had Sooty, Cuddles, Sookie, Smokey, and Smudge. Also, Moany face the little old cat we adopted, who had the loudest ever miaow!

Sooty went missing back in the late 1970s to 1980s, and Cuddles was just young when we lost her due to what we were told was kidney failure.

Sookie, I witnessed getting run over when I was nine years old back in 1982. This was a horrific thing for me to witness as a child; where we stayed, it was not even a fast road.

It was lunchtime from school, and I had gone for a little cycle on my bike while my mum was getting lunch ready. I arrived home, and I saw Sookie out of the corner of my eye. I turned around and was making my way to go and meet her, to pick her up and give her a cuddle, when a car appeared and hit her and ran her over. The driver never stopped; poor Sookie was coming home! I saw everything.

I was even bullied at school for witnessing this — I was called a flat cat. Some other children would run around making car noises and shouting 'splat,' even drawing pictures of a cat killed on the road!

Sometime after Sookie's accident, my sister, dad, and I went to the Dog and Cat Home in Edinburgh. We returned home with a cat — Smokey (she became affectionately nicknamed the tank or fat cat by my brother and me). When my mum saw her, she said oh no, she's a tiger stripe! Smokey was a grey stripey tabby cat, and at the time, she was pregnant — we did not know and were told she was fat, so we put her on a diet recommended by the then vet (mind, this was still in the early 1980s), but I sneaked her little titbits of food when I thought nobody was looking, but my mum knew. Then, one day, my sister saw her tummy moving, and that is when we were told she was pregnant!

Smokey eventually gave birth to 4 beautiful kittens; we kept one named Smudge. They would run up the curtains, run up my mum's legs, full of mischief!

I had just left school at 16 when I was watching television and heard brakes screeching. A man knocked at the door and asked if we had a little tortoiseshell cat as she had just run out in front of his car. He had hit her, but she managed to get herself into our garden. It was indeed Smudge. We took her to the vet, but sadly, her back had been broken, and there was nothing that could be done — Smudge was mum's baby.

Smokey lived until she was 21; she was a happy, affectionate little cat who always greeted us with squeaks and miaows when we arrived home. I remember one day when I was talking to a friend after work at the garden gate when we saw Smokey coming running up the path, meowing hello and wanting a cuddle. I scooped her up in my arms; she loved a fuss and a cuddle. I fondly remember Smokey as she was our longest-living cat and always there. She had been a big part of my life since we lost little Sookie.

We had also adopted a little old cat who chose to come and live with us in her twilight years. She was sitting out in the garden crying one night in the snow. We brought her in for one night — it was meant to be, and she lived with us for another two years before she peacefully passed away. The owners knew she was with us, and we had told them she was at our place and to come and get her, but they did not, so she just ended up staying. Just before she passed, Smokey and Smudge would move for her and let her enjoy the fireplace heat. This little cat called Moany Face absolutely adored my sister and would lie on her like a scarf draped over her. We then had three cats at this point.

Once cats entered my life, my fate was sealed. They became an integral part of my being, and now I couldn't imagine my life without them.

2

My cats and some introduction tips

I adopted my first cats when I moved out of my mum's house and got my own place. They came from the Dog and Cat Home in Edinburgh and were already named Calm and Chaos, names I decided to keep. I was informed they were inseparable sisters and needed to be adopted together. Chaos was a big softie who loved to be close to me and get cuddles, while Calm was more reserved and kept to herself. They were both loving and faithful companions who never wandered too far from my side.

Eventually, I adopted a kitten from a rescue centre in Fife and named her Pepsi, which brought my cat to count to three. Pepsi had a strong personality and was quite stubborn, but my other two cats — Calm and Chaos — were able to accept her. I followed certain introduction techniques during the process, which I will discuss later.

I then also eventually ended up getting another kitten from another rescue centre. I went there with my sister, adopted a cute little kitten, and called him Mo. This brought my total number of cats to four. Calm and Chaos were always together, and they treated Mo as if he were a part of them. However, Pepsi, my other cat, was not as welcoming and often blocked Mo from using the litter tray. I had to keep a watchful eye on him whenever he used the tray, to ensure that he could use it in peace. Similarly, I had to feed Mo separately and gradually move his food bowl closer to Pepsi's until he accepted him. Introducing Mo to Pepsi took a bit longer because they have different personalities. But I was confident that they would eventually get along, and they did.

To introduce Mo to Pepsi, I used gradual introduction techniques, such as scent swapping and keeping them in separate rooms. I let them see each other gradually and made the introduction a positive experience with praise and treats. I also ensured the older cats had access to the house. It is common for cats to see a kitten as less of a threat, and over time, the resident cat will accept the new addition. However, the introduction and acceptance cannot be rushed; it takes time. There will be some hissing, sulking, and growling, but this is normal until the new addition has the 'pack' smell and is accepted. It usually goes one of two ways: they will either love or tolerate each other.

Some introduction tips:

Introducing cats to each other properly, slowly, and carefully is important. Here are some tips to make the process smoother:

- Allow them to get used to each other's scent by swapping towels each cat has been lying on.

- Keep them in separate rooms initially. It's a good idea to have a spare room for the new cat so they get used to each other's scent without direct contact.

- Don't rush the introduction process. Let them take it at their own pace.

- Don't block any exit routes. If they want to leave the interaction, let them go and give them space so they don't feel overwhelmed.

- Keep up with your cat's usual routine so they don't feel left out.

- Once they seem comfortable with this, you can let them see each other through a baby gate or cracked door, for example.

- Gradually increase their time together, but always supervise them if there is tension or aggression.

- Ensure plenty of resources are available (like food bowls, litter boxes, and beds) so the cats don't have to compete for them.

- You can also use pheromone diffusers to help reduce stress and anxiety.

Time passed, and I moved over to West Lothian with the gang. They were introduced to my now husband James's two dogs, Tia and Tori. We took the introductions slowly and carefully; Chaos, Calm, and Mo were OK with it all. They just took it in their stride well, paw steps.

During the first introduction, the dogs were on their leads. As the usual little madam, Pepsi, circled them as if she were circling the wagons. When James went to take them out, she suddenly launched herself. It was as if she had become twice her size. She landed on Tia's back and ran away upstairs!

After that, each introduction got more manageable, and they eventually accepted each other, even lying together (except for Pepsi fluff). We always ensured each of them had a safe space if they wanted to retreat and have peace, and we did not rush the introduction process. We used the same introduction techniques mentioned already but were more careful.

Eventually, Tia would even wash Mo's ears out, and he loved it! He would go and ask her for an earwash! She would look at Pepsi's ears longingly, and Pepsi would look back — 'Yeah, try it,' she seemed to be saying. She ruled with an iron paw and would pass the dogs and look down her nose at them. She would also sit in the middle of the floor, where the dogs would want to get past, and they would look at us and then at Pepsi as if to say 'it's there'… We had to get up and walk past her with them! She would move, and they would run, thinking she was coming for them. One night, we were sitting on the couch with Tori lying at our feet when Pepsi jumped up and casually sidled over, glancing around to see if we were watching. The paw went slowly down; she glanced over to see if we were watching. Slowly, ever so slowly, the paw twitched and whacked on Tori's back. Tori did not know what had happened, and Pepsi had the 'nothing to do with me. I don't know what happened' look on her face. The act of innocence!

Time is precious and slips by much faster than we realise. It's important to cherish every moment and make the most of time while we have it.

Chaos was like a shadow to me. She was just 18 months old when I adopted her and her companion, Calm. Unfortunately, when she turned 16, she fell ill, and nothing more could be done to save her. It was heartbreaking to witness her gradual decline. She had been experiencing seizures and collapses, and each episode took a little bit more of her away from us.

Calm had been diagnosed with hypothyroidism and underwent thyroid removal surgery. However, she still managed to lead a happy and healthy life until she reached the age of 16.5 years. Unfortunately, I had to make a difficult decision to let her go when she experienced a collapse and lost the ability to use her hind legs. It was heartbreaking, but I knew it was the right time.

Then Mr Mo was diagnosed with a heart murmur; he was only 5. We took him to the vet hospital in Edinburgh for further checks, and it was discovered he had cardiomyopathy and was in the stages of heart failure. He was on so many tablets. He went out one day in Aug 2016 and never came back home. We did all we could think of doing: putting posters up, putting the litter tray outside, going out at night when it is quiet, with torches, shaking treats, calling, looking in bushes and shrubbery, asking neighbours, the postal workers, gardeners, and council workers — anyone we thought could help — and even taking the dogs out to see, but nothing. He was also microchipped; nothing ever turned up, and this is now 2024. The not knowing has been the most challenging part.

That led me to set up the Facebook volunteer group *Cats Lost and Found West Lothian* to try and help reunite owners with their lost and missing cats. Sometimes, there is a happy outcome, but not always. At least the owners have the closure of knowing what happened and can grieve and move forward. This group is a volunteer group; the help of the members is what drives it and keeps it going. The more interaction, the more chance there is of the post reaching the owners. Everyone's help is appreciated and welcomed. The group might not be perfect, but we try our best. A vast range of people in the group bring different ideas and resources to help and with varying connections to other people, groups, or charities that can also help.

I had noticed Pepsi was drinking a lot of water and frequently visited the litter tray, so I took her to the vet to see what was happening with her. She was diagnosed with diabetes. The vet asked if I had ever injected or had any experience of diabetes in cats, and I was like, no, with fear in my mind! He said, 'Well then, you are about to learn.' I was shown how to prepare the insulin, the needle, and the injection site. The first time I injected her, I thought I was going to be sick, and I thought she was going to take the needle and inject herself as I was taking so long to do it.

Then it was like the Olympics when it was time to inject her twice a day — over the couch, behind the couch, upstairs, downstairs, over the bed, under the bed, repeat. But eventually, she must have realised this was helping her; she would sit expectantly and wait for her injection and dinner. She was 13 when she unexpectedly took a turn for the worse. I thought she was having a hypo (hypoglycaemic turn), but it was much worse than that, and I had to let her go. She had developed a large mass in her abdomen and had developed anaemia; the decline was so quick and unexpected it happened all so fast; all within 24 hours. This nearly shattered me, as it took me by surprise, and it felt like the end of an era. It was the connection to Calm, Chaos, and Mo, the last remaining bond. I cried non-stop for 24 hours, curled up in a ball, just sobbing. It felt like someone had reached inside my chest and ripped out my heart.

Every time I had to let my cats cross the rainbow bridge, if I could, and if I thought it would have helped, I would give years of my life to give to them.

The house felt soulless, and I was lost. The spark in my eyes had vanished.

A friend told me about a lady who breeds Bengal cats. I did not know what kind of cat I wanted or if I would go to a rescue centre. Anyway, I went to view the kittens as she had one that the reserve had fallen through on, went for a look, and that was me hook, line, and sinker when I saw the kitten. My husband had said not to reserve any as it would not be fair on the dogs as they were old, but my heart ruled my head. I took a picture of her and sent it to him, saying, 'Hello, Daddy.' Oh, it does not end there! I was taken to meet her dad (mum was with the kittens) and then I saw him — he spoke to me (my sister said yeah, he went miaow) — this most handsome lad (who we named Tigger). I asked what his story was as it turned out he had just been neutered as he was an ex-stud cat. The man said he would need to ask his wife if she was planning on rehoming him, but it would probably be a yes.

When I got home, my husband was unhappy that I had reserved a kitten (she's called Lola now), and he asked, 'So when does it come?'

'About two weeks,' was my reply, and I added, 'What is better than one? Two!' My bad. I know. I thought he was going to hit the roof. But he saw my eyes had the spark and life back in them that had been gone. He came with me to pick up Lola and meet Tigger, and he just melted. Lola came home first. The dogs sniffed her, but she was not bothered, and they became friends, even sitting together. We returned for Tigger and brought him home a couple of weeks later. The dogs again were not bothered, and he did not bother the dogs (the lady had a dog, and Tigger had been used to their dog). It was Lola who was not happy with Tigger's presence. The size of her and the attitude, my goodness, but it only took her two days to realise he was a play friend and to accept him; they had a chase and a play, and that was them. Lola is very talkative and likes to shout! Tigger is a daddy's boy and follows his dad everywhere, and I mean everywhere; he sits and waits for him to come home. He is worse than a dog!

If you are making introductions, it takes time, patience, and love and cannot be rushed.

3

Starting up and being self-employed

I have had many varied jobs, but deep down, I always wanted to work with animals. In the past, I have worked in catering, factories, banking, bingo halls, the airport, and care. It is quite a varied bag. I had no idea I would be running my own business and be self-employed back then!

I had heard about cat sitting and thought, what is this all about then? I researched it and learned all that I needed to do. I started small; back in 2014, it was more of a sideline to see how it would go. It has grown to more than I ever dared hope for and taken over my life!

When I started, I had many obstacles; people did not know what cat sitting was — it was still relatively new; I was ridiculed, laughed at, and even told not to bother with it as it would lead to nothing. But also, there was a tremendous amount of support from people who believed in me. I have also had undermining comments saying, 'You won't succeed,' people saying to me, 'They are more a dog person,' 'They don't like cats,' and 'cats are vermin.' The more I was put down, the more determined I was to succeed and prove them all wrong. I am a cat person, and I have made it my job to look after them, which I absolutely love. I followed my heart.

Providing excellent customer service is critical to the success of any business, and this is especially true when dealing with pet owners who are paying for your services.

As a cat sitter, you must be adaptable, flexible, patient, communicate clearly, and have empathy for both the cats and their owners. Effective communication and empathy are essential when dealing with pet owners. You must be able to communicate clearly and effectively with them, explaining your services, answering their questions, and addressing their concerns. Additionally, you must be able to understand their needs and concerns and show empathy towards them. Flexibility is also important when dealing with pet owners, as their schedules and needs may vary. You must be able to accommodate their schedules and be willing to adjust your services as needed. Lastly, patience is critical when dealing with pets and their owners. Cats can be unpredictable, and owners may have specific requests or concerns that require patience and understanding. By prioritising excellent customer service, building a loyal customer base can ensure the success of your business.

As a cat sitter, you must wear many hats to ensure the success of your business. Finding and attracting customers is essential to building your loyal customer base and growing your business. You may need to advertise your services through various channels, such as social media, flyers, or word-of-mouth recommendations. Maintaining a healthy work-life balance is crucial to avoid burnout and ensure that you can provide quality care for your feline clients. Managing your time effectively is essential to prevent becoming overwhelmed, and it's important to set realistic expectations for yourself regarding the number of clients you can handle at once. Getting organised is also important to manage your workload effectively. You need to keep track of your schedule, appointments, and client information, such as feeding schedules and medication requirements. By staying organised, you ensure that you are providing consistent and high-quality care for your feline clients. Lastly, staying focused is essential to providing excellent care for your clients. You must be able to prioritise your tasks, ensuring you are meeting the needs of your clients. By staying focused and organised, you can build a successful cat sitting business that provides high-quality care for your feline clients.

Advantages of being self-employed include the freedom to make your own decisions about what work you take on when you work, and how you run your business. You have complete control over the policies, branding, and clients you work with and can use your creativity to build your business.

Achieving a balanced work-life is essential to maintaining your happiness and fulfilment in your job while ensuring that you have enough time for yourself and your family. This balance can be achieved by having a flexible work schedule that allows you to choose your start and end times. Flexibility in your schedule can allow you to manage your workload effectively while still having time for yourself and your family. You may need to work around your clients' schedules, but finding a schedule that works for both you and your clients can help you achieve a balanced work-life. Having a healthy work-life balance can help prevent burnout and ensure that you are providing quality care for your feline clients. It also helps maintain a positive attitude towards your job and ensures that you are enjoying it. By prioritising a balanced work-life, you can build a successful cat sitting business that provides high-quality care for your clients while also ensuring that you have enough time for yourself and your family.

As a cat sitter, you have the opportunity to earn more by setting your prices and work hours. While it's not guaranteed, you can increase your earnings by building a loyal customer base and providing quality care for your feline clients. Running a business can be incredibly satisfying, especially when you're doing something you love. Seeing your business flourish and your customers happy, you can be proud and feel fulfilled. Additionally, running your own business can give you a sense of independence and control over your career. Owning a cat sitting business can also provide opportunities to learn new skills such as bookkeeping, accounting, marketing, and networking. These skills can be applied to other areas of your life and can be valuable assets in building a successful business. By continuously learning and improving your skills, you can be confident that your business is running well and efficiently. Overall, owning a cat sitting business can be a rewarding and fulfilling experience that allows you to do what you love while providing valuable services to pet owners. With dedication, hard work, and the willingness to learn new skills, you build a successful business that provides high-quality care for your feline clients.

No office politics to deal with: Unfortunately, workplace conflicts are not uncommon, and it can be challenging to deal with such situations. It's important to remember that it's impossible to be liked by everyone, and conflicts can arise for various reasons. Dealing with workplace conflicts requires a level of maturity, patience, and professionalism. Addressing the situation calmly and objectively is essential, without letting your emotions get the best of you. When you have faced workplace conflicts, it's important to remember that such experiences can provide valuable insights or lessons that can help you grow both personally and professionally.

Self-employment has disadvantages: These include the lack of financial stability during uncertain times. For example, when the COVID-19 pandemic hit in 2020, all of my bookings were cancelled, and there were no visits during this period, which meant no income. Although I was still in a full-time job then, it would have been a significant concern for me if I wasn't.

• During periods of low income, as a cat sitter, it's important to plan for periods of low income. Setting aside funds during times of high income can help you get through any lean times that may come up. It's a good plan to have a financial cushion to fall back on. Additionally, it's worth to plan for any unexpected circumstances such as illness. If you become ill and cannot work, you may not receive payment, which can strain your finances. Having a backup plan in place, such as having someone to cover your work during your illness, can help you manage such situations. By planning ahead and having the financial safety net, you can ensure that you are prepared for any situation that may arise.

This can help you provide consistent and high-quality care for your feline clients while also ensuring that you are taking care of yourself and your finances.

As a cat sitter, you may encounter situations where people are relocating from the geographical region you cover. This can be a challenge for your business, as you may lose customers who move away. You may need to consider expanding your service area or doing more marketing campaigns to attract new customers.

Additionally, it's vital to remember that pets can pass away, which can be difficult for both the pet owner and the cat sitter. Providing support and empathy to the pet owner during such times is essential, and handling such situations with sensitivity and compassion is key. As a cat sitter, it's crucial to have a plan in place to manage such situations. You may also need to develop a protocol for handling situations where a pet has passed away, which may involve communicating with the pet owner and providing support and assistance during their grieving process. By being prepared and having a plan in place, you can ensure that your business is equipped to handle any situation that may arise. This can help you provide high-quality care for your feline clients while also building a reputation as a compassionate and supportive cat sitter.

• It's common for some people to use your pet sitting services only once, either to fill in when their regular pet sitter is unavailable or for some other reason. While some people are upfront about this, others are not. However, if you have a solid and loyal customer base, you can accept or decline such one-time jobs. A good working relationship with other pet sitters in your area is always beneficial, as it can be handy in such situations.

People sometimes cancel their bookings; therefore, I have started to take non-refundable deposits. However, I will refund the deposit if the cancellation is a bereavement. Otherwise, the deposit will not be refunded. We waived all cancellation fees during the Covid pandemic, as it was a situation beyond anyone's control.

It is essential to consider GDPR when handling sensitive information. To ensure the security of personal details, all data must be protected by passwords. Paper copies should be stored in a locked safe and then securely disposed of.

If a client requests that their key be kept on file, it must also be stored in a locked safe, either electronically or manually. It is recommended to tag keys for easier identification but avoid including any identifiable information on the tags. When posting pictures, be mindful of what is visible in the background. Do not include any identifiable features, such as transparent images of addresses or phone numbers. Make sure that car registrations are not visible through windows. Always respect the client's privacy, and never share personal information or details with third parties.

Cat sitting is a service where you visit people's homes to care for their cats when they are away. It is a big responsibility that requires trust, discretion, honesty, reliability, and love for animals. It would help if you also were disclosure-checked and insured. It would help if you were prepared for anything and everything that comes your way. Your responsibilities include giving medication if required, making daily drop-in visits — once or twice a day, replenishing the cat's food and water, cleaning the litter tray, and providing love, company, snuggles, and playtime. The amount of snuggles and cuddles depends on the cat's personality. Each visit can last for 15 or 30 minutes, depending on the cat's needs. I recommend at least one visit in 24 hours for the cat's safety, as anything can happen. I have completed various courses and experience as a cat owner. This has given me a greater understanding of how to run a pet care business and provided pet owners with the reassurance that their pets are in safe hands. I possess the necessary pet care skills.

Some of the responsibilities, to name a few:

- Ensuring the security of the client's home is of utmost importance to me. Therefore, when the owner is away, I refrain from posting pictures on social media and limit the use of background images. I take the client's privacy seriously and maintain their home security

- Be prepared to handle any household emergencies that may occur

- Understanding a cat's routine is crucial in providing a sense of familiarity and comfort to both the cat and its owner. By knowing a cat's regular habits, you can create a consistent and reassuring environment that helps the cat feel at ease. This can include feeding times, playtime, and cuddle sessions. Additionally, understanding a cat's individual personality and behaviour can help you tailor your care to their specific needs and preferences. This can help build trust and a strong bond between you, the cat, and its owner

- As every cat is unique, the expectations of each cat owner may vary significantly. Therefore, it's crucial to be adaptable and flexible in your approach to each client. Remember that the cat is the boss, and their needs and preferences should always come first. Being willing to listen to the owner's requests and adjust your care accordingly can help ensure a positive and stress-free experience for both the cat and their owner. Ultimately, a personalised and tailored approach to each cat's care can help establish a strong relationship with the owner and their furry friend

- As a cat sitter, it's crucial to be prepared to handle any medication needs, including administering injections if necessary, to ensure the cat's health and welfare. If the cat becomes ill, you should make arrangements to take them to the vet as soon as possible, while keeping the owner informed of the situation. It's essential to have a good working relationship with local vets and a clear understanding of the owner's preferences in an emergency. Additionally, being attentive to any changes in the cat's behaviour, appetite, or litter box use helps spot any potential health issues early on, allowing for prompt treatment and care. Ultimately, ensuring a cat's health and well-being is a top priority for any responsible pet sitter

- As a cat sitter, it's vital to contribute a clean, comfortable environment for the cat. This includes cleaning litter trays regularly, tidying up any mess, and ensuring fresh food and water are available at all times. Additionally, grooming the cat can help maintain their health and hygiene. Daily updates to the owner, including pictures and videos of the cat, can help reassure them that their furry friend is in good hands and receiving the care and attention they need. Clear communication with the owner regarding their expectations and preferences can help ensure a positive and stress-free experience for all parties involved. Ultimately, providing high-quality care and attention to a cat's needs can help establish a strong bond between the cat sitter, the cat, and its owner

• As every cat is unique, it's essential to tailor playtime visits to meet their specific needs for stimulation. Some cats may prefer interactive play with toys, while others may enjoy solo playtime or simply cuddling and receiving attention. By understanding a cat's individual personality and behaviour, a cat sitter can create a personalised and engaging playtime routine that caters to their unique needs and preferences. This can help keep the cat stimulated, entertained, and happy while their owner is away. Additionally, providing regular playtime can help prevent destructive behaviour to promote a healthy and active lifestyle. Ultimately, understanding and meeting a cat's individual needs is essential in providing high-quality care and attention

The courses I have completed are PDSA Cat Care, Animal First Aid, What Cats Need, Pet Bereavement, Feline Behaviour and Psychology Diploma, Feline Care, and Welfare Level 3: foundation and intermediate cat grooming.

Running a cat sitting business requires much hard work that should not be underestimated. Although it can be very rewarding, it is not as glamorous as some people may think. Especially in the beginning, there is a lot of hard work involved and long hours to be worked, not to mention the administrative work that needs to be done.

To effectively market your cat sitting business, you can use various strategies. Online directories can be helpful as they can give your business more visibility. Networking and sharing your business on online platforms such as social media can also help. Advertising your services in local newsletters, Facebook, Google, and through word of mouth can also be effective. You can follow pet-related pages and groups to connect with potential customers. Having a website, Facebook page, Instagram, LinkedIn profile, email account, and phone number is important. In the UK, you don't need a cat sitter licence, but you will need one if you plan on boarding animals. You can set up a business, get a franchise, or even use an online cat sitting platform. I found that setting up my own business was the best option.

I eventually hired an accountant to take care of my accounts and self-assessments. This gave me peace of mind, knowing everything was being handled properly and accurately. I never enjoyed doing my self-assessments myself.

A considerable amount of paperwork needs to be prepared, such as service agreements, veterinary releases, legal agreements, and other forms like key releases and cat flap disclaimers. You can decide how many forms you want to include. To ensure I had all the necessary forms, I researched what other pet sitters used for their forms. Additionally, I use an app that compiles all the details in one place. The app includes a piece where you can upload a picture of the cat, which can be incredibly helpful if you have many kitties and your business is growing.

To start a business, register it with HMRC as a sole trader. If you run your business from home, you may be eligible to receive money back on your self-assessment tax return. Additionally, keeping track of things like mileage and fuel expense is essential if you use your vehicle for business purposes.

If you're planning on starting a cat sitting business, here are some valuable tips to get you started:

• When setting your pet sitting prices, it's vital to do your research and ensure they are in line with other pet sitters in the area. Attempting to undercut your competition could lead to negative consequences such as reduced service quality for your customers and their pets, running at a loss, and other potential sacrifices. Instead of competing on price, you can stand out by charging slightly higher prices, but be careful not to outprice yourself. To justify charging more than your competition, you can focus on providing exceptional service, going above and beyond for your clients and their pets. This might include offering additional services such as administering medication or providing regular updates and photos of their pets while they are away. In addition to providing high-quality service, it's vital to be transparent about your pricing and the services you offer. Be clear about what is included in your prices and what additional services might cost. This will help your clients feel confident in their choice to use your services and avoid any misunderstandings or surprises. By setting your prices in line with other pet sitters in the area and focusing on providing excellent service, you build a loyal customer base and establish a successful pet sitting business.

To build a successful pet sitting business, it's important to identify what your customers want and do whatever it takes to make your products and services more appealing. Customers want their pets to be well looked after, so charging a higher price for a quality service is better than rushing from one visit to the next. When it comes to cat sitting, the cat will pick up on your vibes and demeanour, so providing a bespoke service tailored to the individual cat's needs is essential. This means prioritising quality over quantity and taking the time to get to know each cat's personality, preferences, and needs. This might include spending extra time playing with a particularly energetic cat, or providing extra cuddles and affection to a cat that is feeling anxious or lonely. In addition to providing high-quality care for their pets, customers also appreciate clear communication and transparency. This might include providing regular updates on their cat's well-being, sending photos and videos, and being responsive to their inquiries and concerns. By prioritising quality over quantity and providing a bespoke service tailored to each cat's needs, you build the loyal customer base to establish a successful pet sitting business.

• Creating a memorable logo is a vital part of establishing your brand and distinguishing your business from the competition. A well-designed logo can grab attention and leave a lasting impression on potential customers. When designing your logo, remember to consider your business's personality and unique selling points. Your logo should reflect these qualities and be able to communicate them to potential customers at a glance. This might involve using specific colours, fonts, or imagery that are associated with your business's niche. Additionally, your logo should be easily recognisable and scalable across different mediums, from business cards to social media profiles to outdoor signage. It should be simple enough to be easily identified, but also memorable enough to leave a lasting impression. Finally, ensure that your logo is unique and distinguishable from others in your industry. This will help avoid confusion among potential customers and establish your brand as a leader in your niche. By creating a memorable logo that displays your business's personality and unique selling points, you can establish a strong brand identity and separates your business from the competition.

• Opening a business account can be beneficial for pet sitting businesses in a number of ways. Firstly, it can make it easier to keep track of finances and separate personal and business expenses. This can save time and trouble when it comes to filing taxes and other financial reporting. In addition, having a business account can give a more professional appearance to potential clients and partners. It demonstrates that you take your business very seriously and are to provide high-quality services. This can help build trust as well as credibility with potential clients, which can in turn lead to more business in the long run. When opening a business account, choose a credible bank or financial institution which offers the services and features you need. This might include online banking, mobile deposits, with account management tools which can help keep track of your finances and stay organised. Finally, it's vital to ensure that you keep accurate records and maintain proper accounting practices. This can help ensure that you are meeting your financial obligations and keeping your business in good standing. Overall, opening a business account can be a smart move for pet sitting businesses looking to maintain organised finances and establish a professional image.

Taking the step towards self-employment can be intimidating, as it means giving up the security of a regular monthly income. It also means being accountable for the success or failure of your own business. Keep in mind that being self-employed has its perks, but it may not be as attractive as it seems.

You never know what you're capable of until you try. Don't let fear hold you back from discovering your true potential. Remember, if you don't try, you'll never know.

4

The Competitors

It's essential to know your competitors in the pet sitting industry. What services do they provide, and how do they market their business? While it's not recommended to copy their literature directly, you can put your unique spin on your services. Remember, you have a different personality that makes you stand out. It's also worth considering building solid relationships with other pet sitters in your area. While some may see them as competition, working together and supporting each other can be one of the most valuable investments you make for your business.

It's always important to consider building solid relationships with your competitors as they can offer a wide range of benefits. You can learn from each other, expand your network, and establish potential partnerships. By interacting with your competitors, you can create a valuable network of contacts who may provide advice, referrals, and more to help you grow and succeed. However, it can be helpful to establish trust and respect with your competitors. You should be open and honest with them and avoid resorting to underhand tactics. Building your business on trust and ethics is crucial, and it will always shine through. Remember, respect and trust are essential in any business relationship. By working together, you can achieve great things and help each other to reach your goals.

Some tips for building relationships with your competitors:

• Building relationships with your competitors can have many benefits. Collaborating with them through joint ventures, development, or cross-promotion might help you reach new audiences and expand your business. Attending any networking events is a great way to meet like-minded people or other business owners who may be interested in your business. However, it's vital to approach these relationships with respect, professionalism, and transparency. Clearly define your shared goals and expectations from the start to avoid misunderstandings or conflicts. Treating your competitors with respect and professionalism could build long-lasting relationships that benefit both of your businesses.

• It can be beneficial for cat sitters to support and help each other. Rather than competing against one another, cooperation can help cat sitters reach more customers and build a solid base. Seeking advice or help from another cat sitter, especially when starting out, can be invaluable. In areas with many cat sitters, it's key to have a good working relationship with them. You never know when you might need their help, and crossing paths is inevitable. By building a network of supportive cat sitters, you can create a community that benefits everyone involved. Sharing knowledge and resources can help everyone improve their services and provide better care for their clients' cats. Additionally, working together can help promote the importance of cat sitting services and increase demand for these services in general. Overall, cooperation is better than competition when it comes to cat sitting. By supporting and helping each other, cat sitters can build a strong foundation for their businesses and provide better care for our feline clients.

I have formed a good relationship with other pet

sitters, namely Tricia from Team Feline — she is a good friend and her help and advice have been invaluable — Andrea from Andrea's Animals, and June from Wee Molly's Pals.

By respecting each other and the businesses we engage with, we foster a positive and productive environment for all. Let's work together to create a culture of mutual respect and support.

5

The customer base

I have laid the groundwork and launched the advertising campaign. Now, I am eagerly waiting for the first customer to reach out to me and help me start building my customer base. It can be nerve-wracking for a beginner to face the first customer. I have prepared everything for the meet and greet, but I am still anxious about whether everything will go smoothly. There are many questions lingering in my mind. Will I be okay? Will they like me? What if I say or do something wrong?

During the meet and greet, I felt a bit anxious, and to be honest, I still am, but I am more confident now. I usually start with a compliment to the owner and not forgetting the cat. This is to ensure that I create a pleasing environment and set a good impression right from the beginning. Don't forget to take all the paperwork with you, including your insurance, disclosure, and agreement forms. It's a good idea to keep them in plastic poly pockets and a folder to make them look more professional and keep everything neat and tidy.

To make the client feel comfortable, it's–important to maintain eye contact. However, staring can be creepy, so avoid doing that. Eye contact is crucial as it helps establish trust, shows that you are attentive and focused, and communicates emotions nonverbally. 80% of human communication is through body language!

If I feel like the conversation might be slowing down, I like to chat about my cats. After all, I'm there to take care of the customer's cat(s), and I want them to feel comfortable with me. We share a common interest, so it's a good way to break the ice.

I understand that the customer might feel anxious and nervous about leaving their cat and house with someone they don't know for the first time. I will show them my disclosure and insurance to establish trust and alleviate their concerns. It's paramount to me that my clients trust me and feel at ease. I treat everyone fairly and like an extended family. I am also very protective of my client's privacy. Handing the keys to your home and everything you treasure is a big deal, so I take that responsibility very seriously.

To establish a strong client base, request reviews, respect their privacy and wishes, and treat them with the utmost respect.

It's important to communicate with the client in an honest and transparent manner. Lying to the client is not helpful, as they know their own cat and house. It can destroy the trust that this business depends on. Keep the client informed with regular updates. If I make a mistake or get something wrong like breaking a bowl, forgetting to put the bin out or setting the alarm off, I apologise and acknowledge the mistake.

It's vital to respect your clients' wishes and maintain professional boundaries. For instance, refrain from messaging them at odd hours and asking inappropriate questions. However, treating your clients like extended family is always a good practice. Sharing your experiences, whether good or bad, helps them see you as a human, not just a machine. For instance, opening up about personal loss, such as losing a pet or a family member, creates empathy and strengthens the bond between you and your clients.

Once you acquire your first customer, you can begin

building and expanding. Learn from errors, ask for feedback, and don't take it personally — grow and learn.

Your customer base is the satisfied customers who become the business's repeat loyal customers and core customers, your bread and butter. They spread the word about your business, they trust you, look after them — you need them! They keep returning to you for your services.

Having a strong customer base depends greatly on providing excellent customer service. It has been estimated that 96% of customers leave a business due to poor customer service. Therefore, it is essential to ensure that your customers feel valued and appreciated by consistently providing great service. This will not only help retain your existing customer base but also help in its expansion. Customers can sense when they are appreciated and always appreciate receiving excellent customer service. So, make sure to keep delivering top-notch customer service to help your business grow and thrive. Your customer base will share with friends or family about any positive or negative experiences, and they will always mention how good or bad the customer service was.

In order to grow your business, it is crucial to have a loyal customer base as they form the foundation of your business. However, it is also viable to have sustainable growth to achieve long-term success. A loyal and strong customer base indicates that you are reaching the right audience with the right products. Having a strong customer base is essential for building a strong business. As a thank you for their loyalty, maybe get or make little gifts; people love to feel appreciated, and it goes a long way. But of course, it is up to you.

You must be adaptable to meet everyone's expectations professionally while being respectful, honest, and discreet. To succeed in any role, it's crucial to be adaptable and professional in meeting each individual's unique expectations. By maintaining a respectful, honest, and discreet approach, you can build strong relationships and foster trust with those around you. Remember, your ability to adapt and communicate effectively will set you apart and help you achieve your goals.

Remember that each client and pet is unique.

Therefore, it's crucial to be adaptable, honest, discreet, and respectful.

6

Kitties, behaviours and socialisation

Now, all kitties are different and fascinating — no two are the same, trust me. They all have their little unique personalities and quirks, much like people.

As someone who provides pet sitting services, I consider myself lucky to have had the opportunity to take care of a wide variety of cats. From the ones who are full of energy to the ones who seem to want to harm me, to the ones who are indifferent and don't seem to care, to the ones who just love to snuggle, I've encountered them all. Over time, I've become adept at understanding each cat's unique personality.

There are many different breeds of cats, each with unique temperaments and personalities. I have encountered various differences among the cats I have owned or cared for.

It's important to monitor your cat's behaviour for any changes that could indicate they are upset, bored, sick, injured, stressed, or frightened. Behaviours can vary, based on individual and breed.

If your cat is stressed or afraid, you might notice them:

- Grooming themselves a lot more than usual
- Hiding
- Sleeping in a hunched-up position
- Changing their feeding and/or toileting habits
- Spraying

If your cat is in pain or frightened, you might also notice them:

- Adopting new, unwanted habits, such as aggression
- Disappearing or avoiding people

If any of these symptoms become an ongoing problem, please contact your vet in the first instance, or if you have any concerns, contact your vet anyway so that any medical issues can be ruled out. If I notice anything that might be 'off' I always contact the owner to let them know or just to check if what I see is 'normal' for their cat.

Some cats prefer solitude, while others need space or confidence. I always let the cat come to me and get used to me and my smell; this is to reassure them I am a friendly face. I will not stress your cat out with attention it might not or does not want. Also, there is a reason I make myself smaller (or try to) by going on all fours, crouching or sitting on the floor. If you seem smaller, it is not as intimidating to the cat, so it does not feel like there is a huge giant looming over them. This is to try and limit or prevent behaviours.

Sometimes, a cat's behaviours can stem from their kittenhood experiences or socialisation. In some cases, traumatic events in their life can also contribute to the development of unwanted or concerning behaviours. Other times, a cat's disposition may be simply due to the way their brain is wired. Despite our best efforts, some cats may remain aloof and indifferent.

The socialisation period (I like the term kitten school), where there is a small window up to around 2-8 weeks, which is crucial in shaping behaviours by helping the kittens to spend time with people and getting them used to people and surroundings. This is a specific time in a kitten's life when the brain and sensory system are still developing and processing external stimuli. This influences how development occurs; everything from who they meet to what they meet will teach them what is happening around them, whether it is threatening or non-threatening.

Positive experiences with different people and different things will teach them of positivity. However, negative experiences, or lack of experience, can cause a kitten to become fearful. If a kitten/cat is good when at 'school,' reward good behaviour with treats (most are food-orientated). If there is naughty behaviour, do not shout, as this reinforces any fear and stress. It is best to ignore negative behaviours and not interact; they soon learn with better experiences.

A kitten's ability to tolerate or even enjoy the company of humans is learned during kitten school. If a kitten is to be confident and happy in adulthood, positive experiences are essential. They learn from mum as well, so it is important mum is not afraid of the 'head human'! Please remember every cat is unique.

There are several things that should be considered during kitten school introductions, including:

- People are all different. They all have different scents that the cat will pick up on, and different age ranges so a kitten can experience such differences. If it were possible, I would make them aware of stranger danger and teach them the Green Cross Code. Unfortunately, not everyone is decent, and roads are bad

- Handling —gets the kitten used to being handled and socialised. This is extremely important to the overall well-being of the kitten and forms a bond by gently touching and interaction creates trust. If a kitten is used to being handled, they will tolerate it more as an adult and it will help you be able to handle them better as they will feel comfortable. It might even help in enabling you to detect any changes in them relating to health issues or if they are hurt

- Sounds —use different everyday sounds, like the vacuum cleaner (some cats will hate the vacuum cleaner, especially if it is loud. You can try and make it a little less scary by letting them investigate it and not chase them around the house with it), the washing machine, conversations, different voices for example. So, the kitten is introduced to them and is not fearful of them, which makes them feel comfortable and reduces stress levels

• Litter trays and types of litter — different cats prefer different trays and litter, find what suits your cat and with which they are happy. You get covered trays, uncovered trays, self-cleaning trays, deep trays, shallow trays, the list goes on. Then the litter — you get pellets/wood pellets, clumping litter, non-clumping clay-based litter, silica crystals litter, biodegradable litter, dust-free litter, scented litter/non-scent, non-tracking litter, paper litter

• Toys — do not use hands, as kittens will think hands are toys and will continue to see hands as toys when they are cats

There can be learned behaviours — learned from mum and their litter mates. They learn how to use the litter tray, play, and interact. Of course, they can learn a lot from us as well. Cats learn from experience. If this is good, they will be keen to repeat it; however, if the experience is an unpleasant one, they will try and avoid it in the future.

Some common behaviours:

Frustration or lack of stimulation: Like us humans, cats can become frustrated or bored if their expectations are not met. For example, If they do not have access to food, play, time outside, or attention, they might exhibit behaviours by scratching the furniture, tail swishing or knocking things over — even aggression. This might be helped by using puzzle feeders, leaving treats around the house, and interactive toys to help the kitty stay engaged and think they are hunting. Even a cat tree might help so they can climb up high to have a vantage point to survey their surroundings.

House soiling: Cats are clean animals. This might be a one-off accident, but if it's repeating, it could be a sign of illness, fright, or litter box aversion.

Perhaps the kitty does not like the litter or the position of the tray (they might like somewhere quiet and private). Maybe they prefer a certain surface to eliminate on or use this as a starting point to recreate the scene, and in the litter, the box gradually starts adding litter. Find a litter your kitty likes and a tray they like. There are so many to choose from. Different sizes of cats may need different size trays, so keep the litter fresh and the tray clean. If there has been an accident, you need to neutralise the odours; if the soiling has been bad, you may need to completely renew the area and place the tray down where the kitty has been toileting. That might just be their chosen spot. Cats usually will not do the toilet in an area where they eat. Try placing some food down in the area (but there is always an exception to the rule). It could be a protest behaviour as well. Perhaps a pheromone diffuser or spray might help. They can be complex little creatures. I know toilet issues can be frustrating and difficult to sort, but there are help and resources. These are just my thoughts on what might help and what I have tried, but please always contact your vet to rule out any underlying health conditions, and they might be able to offer advice.

Toileting issues: Our cats feel vulnerable when going to the toilet (going to the toilet is a completely normal function for the body to get rid of waste products). If there are issues, look at things like is the litter tray in a busy area such as hallway, stairs, doorways or noisy area? The general rule of thumb is one tray per cat plus one. Cats like their eating, drinking, sleeping and toilet areas to be separate. See above for litter trays and litter. Food allergies or intolerances can lead to toilet issues as well. As always, if you have any concerns, contact your vet so any health issues can be ruled out.

Spraying: Cats spray urine to leave a distinct smell marking the territory. They do this by using a vertical object that is in an open location and producing a jet of urine while standing, often padding with the back legs and a tail quiver or two. All cats (yes, all cats) have the ability to spray, whether neutered or unneutered, male and female. This is completely normal behaviour. However, if you have any concerns regarding your cats' behaviours, always seek the advice of your vet so any underlying health or medical conditions can be ruled out.

Aggressive behaviour: It is not often our cats are aggressive towards us, but they do have their limits, and there are several reasons why the cat might become aggressive. If your cat is aggressive, ask your vet for advice. There maybe be a medical reason for aggression. If there is not, ask your vet to recommend you to a qualified behaviourist.

The types of aggression we may encounter include:

Defensive or fearful: Your cat will usually run from anything they think is a threat, but they also may defend themselves if they cannot escape or they have previously learned that fleeing is not or cannot be an option — the fight or flight scenario.

Play and petting: Generally cats prefer short but frequent interactions, which is normal for feline etiquette. In contrast, people often interact less often but more intensely. This can be a bit much for some cats and many have a limit to how much petting they can handle. They could be getting over-stimulated.

Territorial: Usually occurs when two cats meet on disputed ground or when one cat is passing through another cat's territory. They are very protective of their territory.

Pain-induced: Cats suffering from pain may have lower tolerance levels and are more likely to become aggressive without meaning to be.

Cats may be more aggressive if they are:

- Kept indoors without stimulation — they need access to essential resources or a channel for their hunting instinct so they do not become bored
- Young and not aware of the limits yet
- Misunderstood by their owner
- Not neutered — hormones at play

If your cat becomes aggressive, you should always visit your vet so they can check their health and rule out any health-related issues. If no health issue are the cause, your vet may recommend a behaviourist.

You should also consider the common causes of aggression in case there is something about the home environment that is causing your cat's aggression.

Hiding and avoiding: Our cats occasionally hiding is nothing unusual; it is quite normal when they find something might not be quite right; they are creatures of habit. They might hide out of fear or anxiety if they are scared; they will find a hiding spot to feel safe and secure while observing the threat. Loud noises such as fireworks or a new pet being introduced to the household might trigger the hiding behaviours. They might show signs such as wide eyes — dilated pupils, ears flat to the head, they might arch their backs and have their tails tucked in.

Stress or routine: As I mentioned, cats are creatures of habit and love their routine. Even what might seem like a tiny, unimportant change could overwhelm them. If you are implementing any changes, do them slowly and gradually. Some signs to be aware of are sudden aggressive behaviours, being destructive, vocalisation, and inappropriate elimination might also be thrown in the mix.

If they feel unwell or are injured: Cats are masters of disguise and are especially good at hiding signs and symptoms. If they feel ill, they take themselves off to hide to seek a place where they feel safe. If you feel something is not right, look out for changes in your appetite, drinking, litter tray issues, low energy, and or weight loss.

You will know your cat and if you feel anything is not right contact your vet so kitty can be checked over to rule out any medical issues.

Despotic cats — what is a despotic cat? Basically, it is a bully cat, a tyrant, with territorial aggression issues wanting to be the vanquisher, they deliberately go out and seek territory that belongs to another cat, even if that is another cat's home! Eat the cat's food, spray on surfaces and beat the resident cat up (I or rather Calm and Chaos, encountered one such reprobate. They were minding their own business in their garden and this little hooligan came sauntering in and attacked them both, but then there was also another cat that would stick up for my cats and chase this hooligan, standing up to him. Calm and Chaos knew this and would not mind when their friend was about but if they knew the hooligan was around, they would stick to me like glue). They try to intimidate and rule with aggression; they may even turn on the owner if they get in the road. The bully cat usually picks cats that are timid, or old and unlikely to fight back. The despotic cats are usually unneutered tom cats wanting to rule and be dominant.

Overgrooming: Our cats are natural groomers and love taking care of their coat, keeping it clean and pristine. They can spend anywhere up to 50% of their waking time grooming themselves. But sometimes their behaviour can turn into excessive grooming or overgrooming where they excessively lick their fur to the point it causes their skin to become inflamed, sore and resulting in hair loss. Biting might also become involved in this. It may lead to a skin infection. My cat Chaos developed this behaviour of overgrooming and it was a cycle hard to break. She would excessively lick her tummy to the point it was bald and sore, so we had many trips to the vet.

There are two main causes for overgrooming: when the cat starts licking excessively as a form of stress relief (also known as psychogenic alopecia) and medical, with skin allergies or skin parasites being the main culprit to blame. Yes, your cat can get atopic dermatitis. This is an allergic reaction to things like dust and pollen, much like we get with hay fever and allergies. The other skin conditions a kitty might suffer from are flea allergy, dermatitis, and food allergy, to mention three.

Cats, just like us, have skin covering their bodies and sometimes they get skin problems as well, from dry skin, rashes, scabs and sores. Always contact your vet for professional advice if you suspect your cat is suffering from any condition.

The pests like fleas and ticks are also a big factor to consider. It is best to keep these treatments up to date, as prevention can be better than cure. If fleas get into your home, it can be very difficult to get rid of them and it is unpleasant for your cat to have these wee pests. You need to treat the whole house, bedding, soft furnishing; everything and everywhere.

Our home environment can become very stressful for your cat. The stress factors for our kitties do not always register or bother us, but they can cause just as much havoc on them as one of our work disputes or an urgent last-minute job can do with us.

The biggest cause of stress for cats can be other cats — a multi-cat household or other cats in the neighbourhood. By nature, cats are solitary animals and might find living with other cats very stressful. Quite often, this will not show as aggression towards any other cats, and they may happily snuggle up together at home. However, your cat may struggle with the stress, turning to overgrooming as a comforter. (with reference from

Why do cats overgroom and how to stop it, by Amy Shojai on sprucepets.com, also information from Cats Protection and Purina website).

Stressful events for a cat include:

- Moving home (we can get stressed by this as well)

- New furniture (let them sniff it and take in the new smell until they get their scent on it)

Before making a change to your lifestyle, consider if it is likely to affect your cat. These creatures of habit will be the first to react to something new going on in your life. However, the same love for routine can point the way to relieve methods for excessive cat grooming. To assist them in adapting to any changes, offer them things like consistency, hiding places, interact with kitty.

Hairless patches on your cat's coat can be a common sign of excessive cat grooming. However, this is not the only cause why the cat's fur is not as thick as it used to be. Another possible reason is a condition called alopecia or (hair loss) An unhealthy diet or even a hormonal imbalance could lead to your cat losing some of the shiny fur. Your vet will be able to diagnose the condition, understand what is causing it and recommend ways to treat it.

Whatever the cause of their change in behaviour, solving the problem of cat overgrooming can take time. So be patient and work closely with your vet (with reference to *Why do cats overgroom and how to stop it from above note*).

As a cat sitter and cat owner, I have observed a variety of behaviours. It's important to recognise that each cat is unique and has different needs.

7

Pheromones

Pheromones are chemicals released by scent glands all over a cat's body, including the cheeks and paw pads. These chemicals have a unique scent that allows cats to recognise each other. The vomeronasal organ in the front of their mouth helps cats to detect and interpret these signals. It is like a little bump of skin in the roof of the cat's mouth.

Have you ever noticed your cat sniffing areas with their mouth slightly open and making a funny little face? This is known as the "flehmen response", indicating that they are smelling or even tasting pheromones. These pheromones are released and transferred when your cat rubs their face on you or other objects. They communicate a wide range of different messages.

These messages can include:
Cats use scent to communicate in various ways, such as marking their territory by leaving pheromones in their

urine. They also establish bonds or increase familiarity by rubbing themselves on you, leaving facial pheromones. They use their sense of smell to learn about other cats, identify potential mates, and provide sexual signals. A mother cat uses scent to communicate with her kittens. Scent also helps cats identify home comforts, safety, and familiarity. Self-soothing is another way cats use scent by providing a comfort zone similar to when they were kittens with their mother.

Synthetic versions of cat pheromones are available as plug-in diffusers and sprays to help manage stress and anxiety. Always consult with your vet if you have any concerns.

8

Indoor or Outdoor

So, indoor or outdoor for kitty? I prefer the indoor option, but it depends on what is best.

When I had Chaos, Calm and Pepsi, they never went further than the back garden. Mo did have a wander, but he always came back; all my cats were neutered.

Since Mo went missing, I was afraid of the same thing happening again, so when I got Tigger and Lola, we got a catio built in the back garden so they could be safe while getting fresh air and stimulation from outside (A catio is an enclosure built to keep your cat safe. You can furnish it with items to make it more attractive for them and even put in catnip plants!).

The decision to keep our cat indoors or outdoors is pretty much a personal one that depends on various factors. Here are some suggestions for you to consider:

- **The great outdoor desire comes naturally to our cats:**

Your cat has an instinct to explore, and the outdoors is packed with sights, sounds, smells, tastes, and textures they will not find indoors. Some cats are happy indoors, but it is good if you help recreate your cat's natural behaviour at home. To help encourage your cat's natural behaviours is to remember that:

• Cats are hunters and predators — it is in their DNA

The action of stalking and catching something can release 'happy' endorphins in their brains. Indoor cats need a chance to create this 'hunt,' as well. Moving playthings like fishing rod toys and the red dot laser toy can mimic the natural hunting instinct, while puzzle balls and maze feeders will make them 'work' for food, stimulating them.

• Exercise is vital to keep our cats active and healthy — especially for indoor cats. The zoomies are an excellent way for them to exercise, let off steam, and use up some energy.

It is crucial for cats to stay active and maintain a healthy weight. Regular exercise and playtime can help indoor cats burn off extra energy and prevent them from becoming overweight. Activities such as chasing toys, climbing on a cat tree, or using puzzle toys can provide both mental and physical stimulation. For outdoor cats, hunting and exploring their surroundings can help keep them active and engaged. It's great that cat owners take steps to keep their feline friends healthy and happy.

Cats can experience mental health issues just like humans, and it's vital to provide them with an environment that keeps their minds stimulated and engaged. Providing your indoor cat with toys, climbing towers, and activity centres is a great way to keep them active and entertained. However, you should be mindful that every cat is unique and may have different preferences for toys and activities. While you may spend a lot of money on fancy toys and activity centres, your cat might just prefer playing with a cardboard box or a paper bag. The key is experimenting with different toys and activities and finding what your cat enjoys most. This will not only keep them physically healthy but also mentally stimulated and happy.

• Our cat's social life when outdoors versus the indoor cats

Outdoor cats have the opportunity to interact with other cats, which can provide exciting and stimulating experiences that they can't get from their owner. However, outdoor cats also face risks such as fights with neighbouring cats or other animals, exposure to parasites and diseases, and accidents such as being hit by a car. Indoor cats, on the other hand, are more dependent on their owners for social interaction. Providing your indoor cat with plenty of attention, playtime, and affection can help keep them happy and fulfilled. You might also consider adopting a second cat to provide your indoor cat with a companion to play and interact with. Either way, it's imperative to provide your cat with a safe and stimulating environment that caters for their social needs.

If cats are not neutered, an intact tom cat may roam for miles in search of a queen cat in heat. This can put them at risk of getting hurt or killed in traffic or getting into fights with other cats. Additionally, it's worth noting that kittens from outdoor cats can have different fathers. When a queen cat mates with multiple tom cats, each kitten can have a different genetic makeup, with some traits coming from the mother and others coming from different fathers. This phenomenon is known as superfecundation and is more common in outdoor cats that are allowed to mate freely. Neutering your cat can help prevent these risks and ensure that your cat does not contribute to the overpopulation of cats.

• **Outdoor cats can face more significant dangers**

It's crucial to be aware of the potential risks that cats may face when given access to the outdoors. Road traffic accidents are, unfortunately, a common cause of injury and death for outdoor cats, with estimates suggesting that one in four cats die in road accidents, often at a young age, before they are fully aware of the risks. This risk is especially high if you live near a busy road, but remember that it's not always limited to busy roads. Outdoor cats may also face other dangers such as deliberate poisoning, getting caught in traps, or even being stolen. That's why it's a must to weigh the benefits and risks of allowing your cat outdoor access and take necessary precautions to keep them safe. This may include providing a secure outdoor enclosure or keeping them indoors.

• **Indoor living isn't all hazard-free**

Keeping a cat indoors can be a wise decision, as it can offer protection from various hazards that outdoor cats may face. One of the most significant dangers for outdoor cats is the risk of road traffic accidents, which can result in serious injuries and even death. By keeping your cat indoors, you can ensure that they remain safe and protected from such risks, which can lead to a higher life expectancy on average. However, it's worth noting that indoor living can also present certain risks for cats. Cats are curious creatures and may investigate household devices such as washing machines, tumble dryers or dishwashers, and accidentally get closed inside. This can be a dangerous situation for cats, take necessary precautions to prevent such accidents. To keep your indoor cat safe, always check appliances for a napping cat before switching them on. Additionally, it's an idea to check cupboards before closing them, as cats may often sneak inside to take a nap. In many cases, cats will let you know they're there before the cupboard is closed, but it's always better to be safe than sorry. By taking the necessary precautions, you can provide your indoor cat with a secure and comfortable environment that meets their needs while also keeping them safe from potential hazards.

Cats can be little escape artists, and it's vital to take necessary precautions to prevent them from slipping out of the house. While keeping windows and doors leading to the outside closed is the ideal solution, it may not always be practical. In such cases, you might consider cat-proofing the windows and doors with mesh or similar materials to prevent your cat from escaping. However, it's worth noting that even a slightly open window can be an invitation for a curious cat to climb and squeeze out. Cats are incredibly agile and can manage to get into some small spaces that seem impossible. It's almost like they can pour themselves in! Unfortunately, sometimes they can get stuck in such situations, which can be a dangerous situation for them. To prevent such accidents, it's important to keep a close eye on your cat and provide them with a safe and secure environment. If you need to open a window, consider using the lock tilt option, which allows you to open the window slightly while still keeping it secure. By taking these necessary precautions, you can help keep your cat safe and secure while still allowing them to enjoy the fresh air and sunshine.

• **Some cats are better to be kept indoors**

Those kitties suffering from medical conditions such as blindness, deafness, FIV, or elderly cats with restricted mobility with conditions such as arthritis may be better suited to an indoor lifestyle.

Whether your cat is indoor or outdoor, it is recommended to be microchipped with up-to-date details and given annual vaccinations (your vet will advise you on the best one suitable), with flea/tick and worm treatments being kept up to date.

There are also 5 basic animal welfare needs to be met: (I learned more about this when I was completing my cat care courses)

1. Freedom from thirst, hunger, and malnutrition by providing ready access to fresh water and a diet to

maintain full health and vigour

2. Freedom from discomfort and exposure

3. Freedom from pain, injury and disease

4. Freedom from fear and distress

5. Freedom to express normal behaviour

9

The struggle is real and pet bereavement

It is not all plain sailing – well what is?

Weather: This does not always cooperate! One time I was doing a visit when we had really bad snowfall, but the kitties still need to be fed and cared for whatever the weather! It was snowing heavily and had been relentless. I arrived at the visit to find the snow had piled up at the front door. Luckily, I found a shovel that had been left out and dug a passage out so I could get in!

Self-locking doors: These have caught me out! Lesson — always take the key with you if you have to go out of the house, for instance, to retrieve a parcel from the garden. When a self-locking door caught me out, I went to retrieve a parcel that was left, I closed the door behind me —not thinking I would be locked out. I went back and tried to get back in, and then the realisation of what had happened kicked in; I just stood and looked at the door in horror. My keys (all the keys including my car keys), bag and phones were in the house. Nightmare! I had to walk home — it was about a 30-minute walk — wondering how I was going to explain this to the owner. I knew my husband was home and I could get access to my laptop, so I asked him if he could text the owner to explain who he was and what happened; I sent them an email full of apology and asking them whether to get a locksmith. Luckily, they got home earlier than expected and let me know they were home. A rather sheepish me went back up with my tail between my legs. Thankfully, they saw the funny side and were more concerned about my welfare, as my car was in the drive and all my belongings were in the house, but I was not. They had forgotten to tell me about the self-locking door and had been caught out themselves. I had learned my lesson with that one.

Presents: When doing visits, I have been presented with various gifts from our furry friends. I graciously accept and discreetly dispose of them. Your cat considers you family, and as such, views it as their responsibility to provide for you. Also, it is their way of teaching you how to hunt for yourself. Our feline friends are tiny predators, although they have been domesticated for thousands of years, and the instinct to hunt is hard wired into them. They consider you part of their 'pack'. Do they feel sorry for you? Do they want to feed you? Science has not yet figured out why. Although receiving dead animals as gifts is unsavoury at best, it means your cat is happy and healthy and loves you. A cat needs stimulation, especially if they seem to have a strong prey drive; if they do not have anything to 'hunt, chase or catch', then they will find something to fulfil the prey drive. Perhaps pouncing on your feet as you walk by or climb the curtains to catch imaginary prey. For your information, kitties, I would rather have a bar of chocolate as a present. Did you know in times gone by cats were allowed on ships to keep the vermin down and protect the sailors' food?

Oops: Ah, home cameras! I tend to forget about them, since I don't pay much attention to them. However, I have realised that many of these cameras have sound, which means that I unintentionally have full-blown conversations with the cat. I even ask them what they want for dinner, and the list goes on! As a cat sitter, you can expect to spend your time crawling around on all fours, whether it's to play with the cat or clean up after them. I once had a funny occasion when I was checking on a cat. I was wearing a short dress and crawling on all fours while forgetting that there were cameras around. Suddenly, I realised that there was a camera right behind me! I immediately made a note to self to wear trousers in the future. Sometimes, I even wave to my cat if they are sitting in the window.

Illness or loss/bereavement: These situations we come across when the owner is away are thankfully rare; however, they cannot be helped, but when it does happen, it is terribly emotionally draining as we care for your cat like they are our own, and we also have a bond with them. We know how the owner feels. Illness cannot be helped, but you must be aware it can happen and be prepared to deal with it.

I do try to keep myself 'detached' as much as I can. Otherwise, I would make myself ill when a client advises me that their much-loved cat had crossed the rainbow bridge. When loss is experienced, it leaves a gaping hole in your heart; it is so raw.

Dealing with grief: Allow yourself to grieve; grief is grief it's a process you must go through; there are no right or wrong answers. You do what is right for you; it takes time to heal. It is a very personal experience, not a one-size fits all. The stages of grief can come in different stages and in no order; they can range from anger, shock, denial, guilt, depression, and acceptance. There is no rule book, no guidelines, just what is good for you and what works for you. But do not suppress it, as grief, if suppressed, can manifest itself in different ways even years later; accept grief and allow it to come in the order that works for you. I've had the comments that it is just a cat. What does it matter? No, it is more than just a cat; it has been a part of my life; we have shared life moments, new jobs, relationship breakdowns, and ups and downs in life; they have been my witness to life's trials and tribulations while not judging me just accepting me. They have been living, breathing and feeling, a sentient being; they are not an inanimate object.

Some tips that might help with the loss of a pet:

• It is a process you must go through. Do not fight it, but try to accept it

• This is a very personal experience. There are no right

or wrong answers. You do what is right for you

• There are various stages of grief, and they can affect you in separate ways, and there is no order that they come in

• Be kind to yourself

• Remember there are no guidelines or guidebooks for grief

• There are bereavement groups that can help or bereavement councillors; you do not have to deal with bereavement alone

Some people go out and get another pet right away, others choose to wait, and others cannot face getting another pet; it all comes down to what is right for you.

There were two separate occasions in 2023 when I was looking after cats, I had to make arrangements to take them to the emergency (on one occasion, I was waiting 2 hours to be seen by the out-of-hours vet) as they had become unwell and the owner had to make the heartbreaking decision when they were away. It broke my heart on each occasion. As I have experienced this myself, I know only too well what it feels like to let them go. It is important that the client is treated with the utmost compassion and professionalism by us with their little furry family member.

When it's time to say goodbye to your beloved pet, it can be an incredibly painful experience. Your vet will guide you through the process, explain what's happening so you understand that once the final injection has been administered, your pet will pass away within just a few seconds. Your vet will give you some time alone with your pet to say goodbye, and then you can decide whether to opt for burial or cremation.

Euthanasia is a Greek word roughly translated to mean good death, death without suffering.

If doing a visit and you are unsure of any behaviour the cat might be displaying and suspect they might be unwell, always ask the owner in the first instance; if you cannot get hold of the owner for any reason, then contact the vet for advice and be prepared to take the little one to the vet. I have done this on a couple of occasions, but you need to be prepared to pay the bill, and the owner will reimburse you. Some vets may have an arrangement in place, and they will invoice the owner for payment.

Don't be ashamed or afraid of grieving, and don't let anyone make you feel silly or apologise for it.

10

Cuddles and more

I have mentioned that no two cats are the same; they are all different with their different needs, personalities, and traits.

We have encountered some that are just little cuddle bugs and give you the best cuddles and snuggles. You pick them up, and the purr machine has been activated. They just want to give you lots of cuddles; from the moment we arrive, they just want cuddles. Sorry, I mean demand cuddles.

On one visit I did, I left the house with my face covered in hives from the sheer amount of nuzzles, head bumps, and cuddles. Our little friends like cuddles (well some do) as they are bonding with us humans and showing affection as they have a soft spot for us; cuddling is a learned behaviour, and kitties who have been adequately socialised, petted, and handled through the early stages of their lives are more likely to enjoy it. You might even be rewarded with kisses and drool from some.

Genetics can also play a part, and some species, like Maine Coons, Ragdolls and Persians, are naturally more likely to appreciate snuggle time. But again, this is not always guaranteed.

There are also the ones that just fix their gaze on you, and it's like they are looking straight into your soul, reading you and knowing everything about you with no judgement whatsoever, just accepting you as you are. I call them the soul gazers. I think we can learn a lot from our cats from the simple things like live in the moment and enjoy a good nap! They know how to relax, and a lot of their poses and stretches are in yoga stretches!

Now, we also get the ones that just seem to steal our hearts and like to spread the love — how do we know if our cats love us?

It can be the subtle hints to look out for:

• Just being in the same room as you and being near you

• Giving you eye kisses (known as the slow blink. If kitty does this, do it back) also known as slow blinking where your cat holds their eyelids almost closed and seem to wink at you. Cats only shut their eyes when they feel safe, so slow blinking is a sign that they love you and feel comfortable and safe around you. It is a compliment

• Head bumps (also known as bunting) are a sign of trust and affection; kitty is creating a bond and marking you with their scent. Cats use scent to communicate with each other and have scent markings in various places around their little bodies. The scent glands can be found in the forehead, cheeks, lips, chin, pads and tails. So, the next time your cat gives you head bumps, enjoy it, knowing it means they trust and feel safe with you. Do not be confused with the situation where a cat sits and presses its head on the wall; this kind of behaviour needs to be checked by your vet

• Biscuit making — a sign of love and happiness also. Happiness it is completely normal behaviour and goes back to kittenhood when they were kneading their mothers to produce milk. They may knead on a blanket or even on you — it is meant as a compliment

• The fluffy tummy pose — when your kitty is showing you the fluffy tummy, it is usually a sign of trust where the cat is relaxed and feels safe in the environment as the tummy area is vulnerable where the organs are. It is not always a sign to rub the tummy, so be careful. This is sometimes a trap, and your cat does not want a tummy rub as you are invading their space (unless you know your cat enjoys this activity). You will know your cat and will be able to understand their body language

• Purring — Cats purr for various reasons (however, did you know it is not always a sign of happiness?). Cats purr to communicate with their owners and other cats (reference to *Why do cats purr? The science behind the sound* by whycatsdo.org and on Facebook, also Cats Protection at cat.org). When your cat purrs, messages are sent to the vocal cords as well as the diaphragm; this expands when they are inhaling and exhaling. It is an important part of their behaviour and usually a good sign. Purring is a unique vocal activity that cats can produce while they are breathing in and out.

When your cat purrs, it is best to observe their body language and behaviour to determine what they are trying to communicate. If your cat is purring while being petted, it is likely a sign of contentment. However, if your cat purrs while hiding or crouching, this might be a sign of pain, fear or anxiety, as they self-soothe. Studies have indicated that some purring frequencies are so high that it can assist in our cats being able to repair bone, muscle or tissue damage.

As always with some of the subtle hints mentioned, be aware of any changes in your cat's behaviours that could indicate an underlying condition that needs to be checked by a vet.

As someone who both owns and frequently cares for cats, I can confidently vouch for witnessing these particular traits being displayed.

Some of the different characters I come across on visits:

The grump — this kitty just does not like me, no matter what I do or how hard I try. I am in their house, their space, and they are not happy. I have encountered the cats who sit in the doorway growling and hissing (I've also had one or two spitting at me), trying to block my way — sorry, kitty, if you want me to leave, you will need to move as you are blocking the way out. If there is a bit of flesh on show, it's fair game, I have even had to go to visits with horse riding chaps on to protect my legs from swipes and bites! I am sure I can see it in their eyes; they are trying to figure out how to get through to my flesh. Even when wearing knee-high boots, they have been known to go above the boot to have a nibble or swipe. It is probably behaviours, or could it be them showing affection? But also, I know it can be a defensive reaction, as I am coming into their home when their mum and dad are away; they are just protecting their home.

The judge and jury kitties — Tut tut lady, what on earth are you doing? You would never catch me doing that; that is not how my food is served. We need to talk about your culinary and presentation efforts. You can do better. You must bow before me and be ready to serve me. Yes, it can seem like a kitty is judging you and making their own opinions up about you to share with their friends.

Also, the ornamental kitty — you may come into my house, you may feed me, but you may not, I repeat, may not touch me. You may only pet me with your eyes. You may only look at me. I am not here to be petted. I'm just tolerating you being in my home.

Ah, the bossy kitty — who likes to boss us around and boss the other household cats around (if they are a multi-cat household). They like to let us know what they want, and they want it now! We do our best to ensure everyone is treated the same and get their fair share of food and attention.

The nervous kitty — Some kitties are super nervous. They fear everything, even their own shadow, it would seem. We allow these kitties to have their space when we are visiting; we talk to them and let them know we are there. Sometimes, once they start to gain trust and confidence, they will come and see us, gradually coming out of their shell; this is so rewarding when they decide they can trust us.

The drooler — During one of my visits, there was a cat that drooled like a tap running while I was petting it. The amount of drool was quite surprising to me, and I made sure that the cat had not ingested or been in contact with anything it shouldn't have. The owner assured me that it was normal for their cat to drool like that when he was happy and content.

They are just like people — all different, some more tolerant — others not so much.

11

The onward journey

So where is my little cat sitting business now and how is it growing?

It has gone from strength to strength after COVID-19 left its mark, and the lockdowns have been relaxed. With things starting to return to the new normal, people were looking to get a break away and book holidays. My little business started to really take off then. It got to the point I had to take someone on to help me out. This lady was good but unfortunately had a lot going on in her family life and advised me she could no longer help me out, so I had to advertise for someone else. As the nature of the business is very ad hoc —some months are booked solid where other months I can average from no visits a day to 5 — so the hours are not guaranteed. There are 3 ladies now helping me. They are on a self-employed basis, covering my holidays and days off and helping out in emergency situations. Kitties still need to be looked after, and the owners are trusting for this to happen.

As I am constantly looking at ways to improve and grow successfully while keeping my business fresh and interesting, can I add additional services for cat owners to choose from, such as grooming services? It is something I believe that sets my business apart from the competition.

So, what better way to learn? Well, do a cat grooming course!

My friend Jackie and I booked the foundation and intermediate cat grooming course in London. We booked our flights and accommodation full of excitement, wondering what would be in store for us. As it turned out, we had a great time and learned so much! The tutor was very knowledgeable and patient. We got to practise on real cats; these are people's cats that they bring in to be groomed.

We were thinking about what this all could involve — my goodness, we got our eyes truly opened; it is not just a case of brushing (all these years, I've been brushing my cats incorrectly). We have been taught the proper technique, what products to use on the different types of fur and coats and what sort of comb or brush to use. The proper technique of grooming, trimming claws, and what to do if there is an accident and bleeding occurs. And how to clean the eyes and ears properly.

We got to practice on a variety of cats with different coats, long hair, and short hair. Different breeds — Moggies, Persians, Maine Coons, Munchkins, Russian Blue — it was really varied. As we were just learning it was easy cats, we had even then there were a couple of little feisty ones just to keep us on our toes. But we also got a few kisses and cuddles from the cats. If a cat does not want to do something, it is not going to happen!

We can go back to do the advanced and master class course where we will learn different techniques such as clipper and scissor work, which would be interesting to learn, but this gives me the fear, as you are using scissors or clippers on cats and what if they just do not stay still? Some mats can be really tight and almost tied into the skin, and we've heard stories about when someone doesn't know what they are doing, they can accidentally cut the skin or even inadvertently nick an artery! So obviously, we do not do clipper or scissor work, as we have not been trained, and there is no way we are going to attempt this, not a chance.

The cat's skin is quite thin and can tear easily. It has much the same structure as our skin — epidermis, dermis, and subcutaneous layers — all doing the same functions. As with us humans, the skin is the largest organ in the body, providing a protective barrier and helping maintain body temperature. If your cat's coat looks like it is thin, or flaky skin like dandruff, consult your vet so they can rule out any medical conditions.

Should I groom my cat? — Yes, absolutely, it lets you spend quality time with your cat and creates a bonding session. It can help monitor their health and any changes on the body. Grooming removes dust, dead skin, and loose fur. It can help prevent tangling and matting and even reduce furballs.

Should a cat's claws be trimmed? Cat owners usually trim their claws to safeguard the owner and furniture from clawing and scratches. However usually a cat's claws can be left alone unless they are becoming excessively long and causing discomfort or issues for your cat. Of course, if a cat's claws are becoming ingrown and growing into the pad, the claws will need to be trimmed to prevent pain and discomfort for them. You can check your cat's claws by gently applying pressure to the toe, and you should be able to see the claw (you might need someone to hold your cat if they are not very compliant!) The claw should be showing with no signs of loose bits from shedding. Sometimes, you might see the claw sheath that's been shed. This is completely normal, as much like our nails, the cat's claws are made of keratin and constantly growing. The sheath is the dead part that has come off and there will be a new claw in the cat's paw. A cat can also take care of their own claws when they groom themselves, also different textures and surfaces that your cat encounters can help with claw maintenance; you can also try scratching furniture like scratching posts, cardboard scratchers, sisal (sisal is made from the fibres of the agave plant and woven together to create a rope effect — a great natural product). I have put catnip on the items to try and encourage my cats to use them rather than the carpets and furniture! In my personal experience my cats prefer the cardboard scratchers, but every cat is different with their own preferences.

How can I tell if my cat is uncomfortable with the

grooming session? They give off little subtle signs, so it is advisable to familiarise ourselves with the signs:

• tail twitching/swishing

• ears flattening

• pupils dilating

• panting

Recognise these signs and stop the grooming. It will help reduce the risk of more serious warnings; try and read your cat's body language. If you notice the point at which your cat's demeanour changes, take note of this and stop the groom prior to this, as they have a point they reach, and that is enough. We want the kitty to enjoy the groom and see it as something positive; all cats are different. Some will let you groom them all day, some will tolerate it, and others will be like no chance. We will not stress your cat; if it shows signs of distress, we stop the groom immediately. We want the groom to be a positive and enjoyable experience, not one your cat will dread.

If you are thinking about trying something that will enhance your business and add to your knowledge, then go ahead, try it. You never know where it may take you.

About the Author

Jillian S. Brown, I'm a hardworking and passionate author from Edinburgh. I was born in 1973, and brought up with a strong work ethic, which has served me well throughout my career.

I'm the youngest of three children and have always loved reading books. I enjoy a variety of genres, with John Grisham's books being my personal favourite. My journey to becoming an author has been a long and varied one, having worked in several industries such as factories, financial sectors, and care. However, I have finally found my true calling in cat sitting.

I reside in Edinburgh with my husband and two cats. Apart from reading and writing, I enjoy baking, practising yoga, and spending time with my cats. I'm a massive cat lover and understand the importance of having pets in your life.

My diverse work experience has helped me develop a unique perspective, which is reflected in my writing. With my debut book on the horizon, the journey to becoming a published author is one that readers will not want to miss!

www.blossomspringpublishing.com